The Process

Strategies To Obtaining Home Loan Approval

Elder

Anna Marie Wilson

Publishing Services By: Ms. Annette Morris / Goal Getter LLC

Library of Congress Cataloging – in- Publication Data has been applied for.

Ppaerback ISBN: 979-8-9859916-4-2
Ebook ISBN: 979-8-9859916-5-9

PRINTED IN THE UNITED STATES OF AMERICA.

First Edition

PRAYER

In my world, everything begins and ends with prayer; it is the only consistent thing that works in my life.

Spirit of the Living God, we thank you for everyone who has a desire to move to the next level in life. For everyone who wants the knowledge to progress. For Everyone who takes the time to obtain wisdom, clarity, and understanding.

Father, thank you for allowing us the ability to desire better, to accomplish, and to move toward better, for we understand that in and through you, all things are possible.

Our prayer is that everyone who opens this book is educated, empowered, and encouraged to get their credit to begin a budget and take steps to move forward in becoming brand new homeowners and investors.

We bind up the spirit of fear which holds us in bondage
Father, we lose down your spirit of victory in their lives now in the Name of Jesus.

Amen

ENDORSEMENTS

Anna was such an immense help to us in purchasing our first home. She was patient and knowledgeable of what we needed to do and how we needed to accomplish it. She worked the numbers and found us grant money also found through looking at the tax returns that we had a refund due to us by filling our taxes correctly. We are forever grateful to her.
We thought we could not purchase it. She never once said no; she only said, let's find out how to make this happen.

~Benjamin & Nicole Clay

Anna, better known to many of us as Elder Anna is a sweetheart and excellent person. She is always willing to help when someone needs help, no matter what. She is dedicated to helping people realize their dream of homeownership. When purchasing my home, she walked me through my process step by step; she was supportive and patient. Elder Anna, keep up the excellent work. God indeed sends you to help others.

~Perica Brown

I was a first-time homebuyer, and I can say it was tough, but with Ms. Anna's knowledge and dedication, the process was exceptional and rewarding. Ms. Anna told me precisely what I needed to do with my credit when my score went down in the middle of the process, but everything still worked out perfectly. She did not panic. Ms. Anna makes sure she goes the extra mile; Ms. Anna is devoted, trustworthy, fun, and excellent at what she does; she makes the home buying experience comfortable and easy. Please complete the same choice I did and go with her, you will not be disappointed!!! I live in my dream home!!!! Thanks a bunch!!!!

~Candace Williams

DEDICATION

The dedication of this book is to the Father first and above all who has kept me through 37 years of being in the Real Estate and Mortgage industry. I am grateful and humble for each experience through the tuff seasons and the extraordinary seasons.

To every Realtor who over the last 37 years entrusted me with helping their clients to become homeowners, thank you. I could not name you all; it would be a book within itself.

To every employer especially Mrs. Carol Johnson, who took me and trained me to be one of the ones doing mortgages the right way and instilling in me to always know the guidelines and to operate by them to be one of the best. Thank you, Carol; you were so hard on me, but I now understand that it helped make me the person I am in the mortgage industry.

To every Borrower, thank you for allowing me to be a part of your dreams and visions. For every referral you have sent back over the years, I genuinely appreciate every one of you.

To my children, who had understood when Mommy had to work late and work on weekends at times. For understanding when the work was overwhelming, I bought home the frustrations of everyday mortgage stuff.

I love each of you individually and collectively.

To the man who has sent my Husband Rynell Wilson, thank you for the encouraging words in every project and every assignment that God has given me.

Love you, Sir, for all eternity.

I will never forget my Publisher Ms. Annette Morris / Goal Getter LLC, for never giving up on me, I have to remind her to be nice when we have our meetings, and she says where is the work I assigned. LOL everyone needs a pusher in their life to make sure you are constantly moving to higher levels.

Love you, lady

TABLE OF CONTENTS

Message From The Author 1

Yes, You Can, So Let's Get Started! 3

The Process That Helps Make Dreams Come True!!! 5

Frequently Asked Questions 7

Down Payments 8

Gathering Your Information 10

Uniform Residential Loan Application (1003) 16

Analyze Your Thoughts 21

Making The Call 23

Your Identity 25

Accounts 27

Income Verification 29

Tax Returns 30

Negotiating The Purchase Contract Is The Next Step In Your Process 32

About The Author 36

MESSAGE FROM THE AUTHOR

I have been in the Mortgage / Real Estate industry for over 37 years now, and I have seen the industry go up, and I've seen it go down; in my opinion, everyone deserves a chance at homeownership. However, you must be willing to work and maintain your credit, money, and new home. For sure, if you never begin, you will never finish, you must make the first step and then proceed to the finish line, but like everything in life, it is a process.

If you have FAITH and do the work, you can accomplish anything, but only if you get in a position to start.

If you do not start, you will never know what position you are in. Be persistent at all costs and push till your visions and dreams become your reality.

QUESTION?
How bad do you want to accomplish this task?

Hosea 4:6 says – My people parish for a lack of knowledge
Delay is just that it is not denial it simply means you have some work to do before the approval. This will depend on how bad you want to become a HOMEOWNER or INVESTOR of real estate.

Whether you are a purchaser or currently own your own home and simply want to refinance, the rules will apply.

We speak of breaking generational curses and changing our mindset about money and credit. We shall be a generation leaving an inheritance of wealth for our children. Please understand Real Estate is wealth when you make a sound, informed decision. We should be educating and teaching our children about homeownership & building wealth; yes, again, I say wealth owning Real Estate.

Taking the time to research and find out precisely what you need to do to become a new homeowner or investor or refinancing and pulling out cash is very important.

Getting with the right team that fits your needs will keep you encouraged and your mind focused on the task at hand. It would help if you did not lose focus or get distracted.
Question?

1. What is your mindset?
2. What are your goals?
3. What is your time frame?
4. What do you need to do to accomplish the task?

Refinancing:

There are several reasons you may want to refinance your home,
1. Lower your interest rate
2. Take cash out to invest in something.
3. Pay off current debts.
4. Take vacations
5. Whatever your goal may be, a refinance can most likely help you accomplish it.
6. Note that you must have equity in the property to accomplish a refinance, and credit must be in good standing NO late payments on the mortgage in the last 12 months.

I am sure this publication will help you accomplish your goal regarding intelligent and wise decisions on dealing in the Real Estate world.

Proverbs 4:7 Wisdom is the principal thing; therefore, get wisdom: with all thy getting an understanding.

Anna Marie Wilson

YES, YOU CAN, SO LET'S GET STARTED!

Know your Goal
What are your goals?
Be specific in what your goals are.
Habakkuk 2: 2-3 Write the vision, make it plain so that he who sees it may run with it, For still, the vision awaits its appointed time.

_____

_____

_____

_____

_____

_____

_____

_____

_____

_____

_____

_____

_____

_____

_____

_____

_____

_____

THE PROCESS THAT HELPS MAKE
DREAMS COME TRUE!!!

This publication is being produced by Bent but Not Broken LLC. CEO is Anna Marie Wilson; she has been serving the community for over 37 years in the home buying process, helping others to realize their dreams of homeownership.

The manual will give you a complete understanding of the home buying process step by step. It will explain the what's, the why's, and the how's. It will help you to know if homeownership is right for you at this time or should you wait and do some more preparation work before taking the next step.

Everything the lender asks you to provide has a reason and a purpose; you should give them exactly what they are requesting, precisely the way they ask you for the items, do not try and change things to fit what you think they should be asking for; you will delay your process.
(Make sure you understand every question that is asked, if you do NOT understand, stop them and ask for clarity) it is their job to make you comfortable and make sure you are fully aware of what is happening and why.

We will go through the process of beginning your process & preparing you to make your application from start to finish.

If we miss anything you come up against & need clarification, don't hesitate to contact us. Our contact information is bentbutnotbroken2014@gmail.com we will repeat at the end of this publication.

Remember that the application and meeting with a lender should be your first step, not the 2nd or 3rd. You must know your buying power or lack thereof before meeting a realtor so they will take you seriously. They will ask about a pre-approval or pre-qualify letter; the only way to have that is to meet with the lender first.

Remember, they are not tour guides; this is their business; livelihood and they are highly trained in the real estate market.

THE PROCESS

We will touch on the guidelines that the mortgage industry must follow. Some are most common because this publication can't have everything. Still, we promise it will give you an excellent reference guide to follow and an excellent understanding of the process. Please keep in mind the mortgage industry is constantly changing daily, sometimes hourly.

I pray that the information within these pages will give you an excellent understanding of the process; please keep in mind that things change absolutely every day in the mortgage industry.

FREQUENTLY ASKED QUESTIONS

1. What does my credit score have to be?
2. How long will it take to increase my score?
3. What is the difference between Fico and Vantage scores?
4. What is the difference between a Mortgage company and a bank?
5. What role does the Lenders play?
6. Why is my past credit so important? It should only matter what I'm doing now.
7. Why are you removing the disputes from my credit? I was told that would help my score.
8. How does bankruptcy affect my credit and my buying power? Can it affect me in any way?
9. How long before I can purchase after I have filed for bankruptcy?
10. Why can't I use my second income to qualify? I took this job to help me prepare.
11. Can I use my child support?
12. Can I buy a property that needs repairs?
13. WHY DO I NEED A REALTOR?

DOWN PAYMENTS

Federal Housing Administration (FHA), 3.5% down payment

FHA 203K (Rehabilitation Loan) 3.5% down payment

Veterans Administration (VA), No down payment 100% financing

Fannie Mae (CNV), as low as 3% down depending on program and scores, investing 20% + depending on the program.

USDA (Rule Development) No down payment 100% financing (ONLY FOR RULE Area's) Non-Conforming higher rates large down payments depending on credit scores and loan programs.

Some of this may hurt, but I promise it will bless your life and get you ready to move to the next level in your life.

VERY IMPORTANT NUGET

If you are ready, let's get started – During your process, don't compare your approach to anyone else's process. Because you do not know their credit history or financial situation, you only know what they may tell you and what they may leave out. Every deal is uniquely different.

DO NOT RELY ON THE CREDIT APPS THAT ARE OUT; THEY NORMALLY DO NOT CARRY FICO SCORES, OR THEY ARE NOT CORRECT.

LET'S BEGIN THE GATHERING OF INFORMATION IS VERY IMPORTANT TO BE TRANSPARENT WITH YOUR LOAN SPECIALIST

- Valid Driver's License and Social Security Card
- Last 2 years complete tax returns (ALL pages)
- Previous 2 years w's forms (ALL Jobs)
- Last 2 paycheck stubs Last 30 days
- Last 2 months bank statements
- IRA Account, Retirement Accounts that you can pull cash out of.
- Documents for all Annuities and Royalties

- Current Social Security & Retirement Awards letter
- Child Supports court order document. Proof you have received if for the last 3 months and Birth certificates
- All documentation such as the court-ordered judgment
- VA Eligibility Certificate
- Self Employed P&L & CPA Letter on how long you have been in business and that you are still in business.

IF YOU HAVE EVER FILED BANKRUPTCY:

You will need the full bankruptcy schedules along with the discharge papers. If you do not have them, you must obtain them.

Official court copies of bankruptcy records are available from all Federal Bankruptcy Courts in the United States. Cases are typically emailed within 10 minutes but always within an hour. Copies are compliant with all lenders, creditor, and credit reporting agency requirements. If you have questions or require assistance, please call a clerk at 866-780-5901. (per Google search)

ASSETS:

Know where your MONEY to close your loan is coming from to make your transaction happen.

Every penny must be documented, and the origin of the funds will need to be proven. From Placing your deposit, paying for the inspections & appraisal fees to closing the actual deal.

DO NOT USE CASH USE TRACKABLE FUNDS!!!

NO SUCH THING AS NOT NEEDING ANY MONEY!

ACCEPTABLE SOURCE OF FUNDS $$$$

Bank account (savings or checking)

IRA, CD's, Retirement Fund / 401k

Grant Money, Gift Funds, Tax Return Refund, Equity

Bonus from your employer

Will the Seller pay any of the cost for you? (Ask)

FHA they can pay up to 6%

VA they can pay up to 4%

Conventional they can pay up to 3%

GATHERING YOUR INFORMATION

When collecting your information, bring everything to be transparent; they cannot help you if they don't know.

- Last 2 years federal tax returns (ALL PAGES)
- You must know what is on your returns and why there are tax write-offs on your return if you are not self-employed (critical)
- Last 2 w'2 forms (FOR ALL JOBS IN THE LAST 2 YEARS)
- If self-employed current YTD profit & loss
- CPA letter stating you have been in business for the last 5 years or better, also if you are still operating. This is not a tax preparer, it has to be done by a Certified Public Accountant.
- If on Social Security your awards letter
- Last 2 pay stubs, unless you are paid every week, then you need last 30 days
- Know your deductions on your check stubs, explain them, & document any deductions that are not normal.
- Retirement award letter
- Proof of child support, the judgments, and printouts showing you have been receiving the child support
- Last 2 bank statements with full explanations and documentation on any large deposits
- 401k statements
- Last 2 years rental history
- Last 2 years of employment
- Valid Driver's License
- Social Security Card
- Know where your money will come from to purchase your home.
- Full bankruptcy papers & Discharge (very important)
- Call a Mortgage Lender and obtain a Pre-Approval
- HONESTY is the best policy, not to waste your time or theirs.
- Call a licensed Realtor (Don't try to do this on your own)
- Time to get acquainted with a 1003

Uniform Residential Loan Application

This application is designed to be completed by the applicant(s) with the Lender's assistance. Applicants should complete this form as "Borrower" or "Co-Borrower," as applicable. Co-Borrower information must also be provided (and the appropriate box checked) when ☐ the income or assets of a person other than the Borrower (including the Borrower's spouse) will be used as a basis for loan qualification or ☐ the income or assets of the Borrower's spouse or other person who has community property rights pursuant to state law will not be used as a basis for loan qualification, but his or her liabilities must be considered because the spouse or other person has community property rights pursuant to applicable law and Borrower resides in a community property state, the security property is located in a community property state, or the Borrower is relying on other property located in a community property state as a basis for repayment of the loan.

If this is an application for joint credit, Borrower and Co-Borrower each agree that we intend to apply for joint credit (sign below):

Borrower _____   Co-Borrower _____

I. TYPE OF MORTGAGE AND TERMS OF LOAN

Mortgage Applied for:	☐ VA ☐ FHA	☐ Conventional ☐ USDA/Rural Housing Service	☐ Other (explain):	Agency Case Number	Lender Case Number
Amount $	Interest Rate %	No. of Months	Amortization Type:	☐ Fixed Rate ☐ GPM	☐ Other (explain): ☐ ARM (type):

II. PROPERTY INFORMATION AND PURPOSE OF LOAN

Subject Property Address (street, city, state & ZIP)		No. of Units
Legal Description of Subject Property (attach description if necessary)		Year Built

Purpose of Loan	☐ Purchase ☐ Construction ☐ Other (explain): ☐ Refinance ☐ Construction-Permanent	Property will be: ☐ Primary Residence ☐ Secondary Residence ☐ Investment

Complete this line if construction or construction-permanent loan.

Year Lot Acquired	Original Cost $	Amount Existing Liens $	(a) Present Value of Lot $	(b) Cost of Improvements $	Total (a + b) $ 0.00

Complete this line if this is a refinance loan.

Year Acquired	Original Cost $	Amount Existing Liens $	Purpose of Refinance	Describe Improvements ☐ made ☐ to be made
				Cost: $

Title will be held in what Name(s)	Manner in which Title will be held	Estate will be held in: ☐ Fee Simple ☐ Leasehold (show expiration date)
Source of Down Payment, Settlement Charges, and/or Subordinate Financing (explain)		

III. BORROWER INFORMATION

Borrower	Co-Borrower
Borrower's Name (include Jr. or Sr. if applicable)	Co-Borrower's Name (include Jr. or Sr. if applicable)

Social Security Number	Home Phone (incl. area code)	DOB (mm/dd/yyyy)	Yrs. School	Social Security Number	Home Phone (incl. area code)	DOB (mm/dd/yyyy)	Yrs. School

☐ Married ☐ Unmarried (include ☐ Separated single, divorced, widowed)	Dependents (not listed by Co-Borrower) no. ages	☐ Married ☐ Unmarried (include ☐ Separated single, divorced, widowed)	Dependents (not listed by Borrower) no. ages
Present Address (street, city, state, ZIP) ☐ Own ☐ Rent ___ No. Yrs.		Present Address (street, city, state, ZIP) ☐ Own ☐ Rent ___ No. Yrs.	
Mailing Address, if different from Present Address		Mailing Address, if different from Present Address	

If residing at present address for less than two years, complete the following:

Former Address (street, city, state, ZIP) ☐ Own ☐ Rent ___ No. Yrs.		Former Address (street, city, state, ZIP) ☐ Own ☐ Rent ___ No. Yrs.	

IV. EMPLOYMENT INFORMATION

Borrower	Co-Borrower

Name & Address of Employer	☐ Self Employed	Yrs. on this job	Name & Address of Employer	☐ Self Employed	Yrs. on this job
		Yrs. employed in this line of work/profession			Yrs. employed in this line of work/profession
Position/Title/Type of Business	Business Phone (incl. area code)		Position/Title/Type of Business	Business Phone (incl. area code)	

If employed in current position for less than two years or if currently employed in more than one position, complete the following:

Borrower			IV. EMPLOYMENT INFORMATION (cont'd)	Co-Borrower		
Name & Address of Employer	☐ Self Employed	Dates (from – to)	Name & Address of Employer	☐ Self Employed	Dates (from – to)
		Monthly Income $			Monthly Income $
Position/Title/Type of Business	Business Phone (incl. area code)		Position/Title/Type of Business	Business Phone (incl. area code)
Name & Address of Employer	☐ Self Employed	Dates (from – to)	Name & Address of Employer	☐ Self Employed	Dates (from – to)
		Monthly Income $			Monthly Income $
Position/Title/Type of Business	Business Phone (incl. area code)		Position/Title/Type of Business	Business Phone (incl. area code)

V. MONTHLY INCOME AND COMBINED HOUSING EXPENSE INFORMATION

Gross Monthly Income	Borrower	Co-Borrower	Total	Combined Monthly Housing Expense	Present	Proposed
Base Empl. Income*	$	$	$ 0.00	Rent	$	
Overtime			0.00	First Mortgage (P&I)		$
Bonuses			0.00	Other Financing (P&I)		
Commissions			0.00	Hazard Insurance		
Dividends/Interest			0.00	Real Estate Taxes		
Net Rental Income			0.00	Mortgage Insurance		
Other (before completing, see the notice in "describe other income," below)			0.00	Homeowner Assn. Dues		
				Other:		
Total	$ 0.00	$ 0.00	$ 0.00	Total	$ 0.00	$ 0.00

* Self Employed Borrower(s) may be required to provide additional documentation such as tax returns and financial statements.

Describe Other Income   *Notice:* Alimony, child support, or separate maintenance income need not be revealed if the Borrower (B) or Co-Borrower (C) does not choose to have it considered for repaying this loan.

B/C		Monthly Amount
		$

VI. ASSETS AND LIABILITIES

This Statement and any applicable supporting schedules may be completed jointly by both married and unmarried Co-Borrowers if their assets and liabilities are sufficiently joined so that the Statement can be meaningfully and fairly presented on a combined basis; otherwise, separate Statements and Schedules are required. If the Co-Borrower section was completed about a non-applicant spouse or other person, this Statement and supporting schedules must be completed about that spouse or other person also.

Completed ☐ Jointly ☐ Not Jointly

ASSETS Description	Cash or Market Value	Liabilities and Pledged Assets. List the creditor's name, address, and account number for all outstanding debts, including automobile loans, revolving charge accounts, real estate loans, alimony, child support, stock pledges, etc. Use continuation sheet, if necessary. Indicate by (*) those liabilities, which will be satisfied upon sale of real estate owned or upon refinancing of the subject property.		
Cash deposit toward purchase held by:	$			
List checking and savings accounts below		**LIABILITIES**	**Monthly Payment & Months Left to Pay**	**Unpaid Balance**
Name and address of Bank, S&L, or Credit Union		Name and address of Company	$ Payment/Months	$
Acct. no.	$	Acct. no.		
Name and address of Bank, S&L, or Credit Union		Name and address of Company	$ Payment/Months	$
Acct. no.	$	Acct. no.		
Name and address of Bank, S&L, or Credit Union		Name and address of Company	$ Payment/Months	$
Acct. no.	$	Acct. no.		

VI. ASSETS AND LIABILITIES (cont'd)

Name and address of Bank, S&L, or Credit Union		Name and address of Company	$ Payment/Months	$
Acct. no.	$	Acct. no.		
Stocks & Bonds (Company name/ number & description)	$	Name and address of Company	$ Payment/Months	$
		Acct. no.		
Life insurance net cash value	$	Name and address of Company	$ Payment/Months	$
Face amount: $				
Subtotal Liquid Assets	$ 0.00			
Real estate owned (enter market value from schedule of real estate owned)	$			
Vested interest in retirement fund	$			
Net worth of business(es) owned (attach financial statement)	$	Acct. no.		
Automobiles owned (make and year)	$	Alimony/Child Support/Separate Maintenance Payments Owed to:	$	
Other Assets (itemize)	$	Job-Related Expense (child care, union dues, etc.)	$	
		Total Monthly Payments	$	
Total Assets a.	$ 0.00	Net Worth (a minus b) ▶ $ 0.00	**Total Liabilities b.**	$ 0.00

Schedule of Real Estate Owned (If additional properties are owned, use continuation sheet.)

Property Address (enter S if sold, PS if pending sale or R if rental being held for income) ▼	Type of Property	Present Market Value	Amount of Mortgages & Liens	Gross Rental Income	Mortgage Payments	Insurance, Maintenance, Taxes & Misc.	Net Rental Income
		$	$	$	$	$	$
Totals		$ 0.00	$ 0.00	$ 0.00	$ 0.00	$ 0.00	$

List any additional names under which credit has previously been received and indicate appropriate creditor name(s) and account number(s):

Alternate Name	Creditor Name	Account Number

VII. DETAILS OF TRANSACTION		VIII. DECLARATIONS				
a. Purchase price	$	If you answer "Yes" to any questions a through i, please use continuation sheet for explanation.	Borrower		Co-Borrower	
			Yes No		Yes No	
b. Alterations, improvements, repairs		a. Are there any outstanding judgments against you?	☐ ☐		☐ ☐	
c. Land (if acquired separately)		b. Have you been declared bankrupt within the past 7 years?	☐ ☐		☐ ☐	
d. Refinance (incl. debts to be paid off)		c. Have you had property foreclosed upon or given title or deed in lieu thereof in the last 7 years?	☐ ☐		☐ ☐	
e. Estimated prepaid items		d. Are you a party to a lawsuit?	☐ ☐		☐ ☐	
f. Estimated closing costs		e. Have you directly or indirectly been obligated on any loan which resulted in foreclosure, transfer of title in lieu of foreclosure, or judgment?	☐ ☐		☐ ☐	
g. PMI, MIP, Funding Fee		(This would include such loans as home mortgage loans, SBA loans, home improvement loans, educational loans, manufactured (mobile) home loans, any mortgage, financial obligation, bond, or loan guarantee. If "Yes," provide details, including date, name, and address of Lender, FHA or VA case number, if any, and reasons for the action.)				
h. Discount (if Borrower will pay)						
i. Total costs (add items a through h)	0.00					

<table>
<tr><td colspan="2">VII. DETAILS OF TRANSACTION</td><td colspan="5">VIII. DECLARATIONS</td></tr>
</table>

VII. DETAILS OF TRANSACTION		VIII. DECLARATIONS	Borrower		Co-Borrower	
		If you answer "Yes" to any questions a through i, please use continuation sheet for explanation.	Yes No		Yes No	
j.	Subordinate financing					
k.	Borrower's closing costs paid by Seller	f. Are you presently delinquent or in default on any Federal debt or any other loan, mortgage, financial obligation, bond, or loan guarantee? If "Yes," give details as described in the preceding question.	☐ ☐		☐ ☐	
l.	Other Credits (explain)	g. Are you obligated to pay alimony, child support, or separate maintenance?	☐ ☐		☐ ☐	
		h. Is any part of the down payment borrowed?	☐ ☐		☐ ☐	
m.	Loan amount (exclude PMI, MIP, Funding Fee financed)	i. Are you a co-maker or endorser on a note?	☐ ☐		☐ ☐	
		j. Are you a U.S. citizen?	☐ ☐		☐ ☐	
n.	PMI, MIP, Funding Fee financed	k. Are you a permanent resident alien?	☐ ☐		☐ ☐	
		l. Do you intend to occupy the property as your primary residence? If "Yes," complete question m below.	☐ ☐		☐ ☐	
o.	Loan amount (add m & n) 0.00	m. Have you had an ownership interest in a property in the last three years?	☐ ☐		☐ ☐	
p.	Cash from/to Borrower (subtract j, k, l & o from i)	(1) What type of property did you own—principal residence (PR), second home (SH), or investment property (IP)? _____ (2) How did you hold title to the home—solely by yourself (S), jointly with your spouse (SP), or jointly with another person (O)? _____			_____ _____	

IX. ACKNOWLEDGEMENT AND AGREEMENT

Each of the undersigned specifically represents to Lender and to Lender's actual or potential agents, brokers, processors, attorneys, insurers, servicers, successors and assigns and agrees and acknowledges that: (1) the information provided in this application is true and correct as of the date set forth opposite my signature and that any intentional or negligent misrepresentation of this information contained in this application may result in civil liability, including monetary damages, to any person who may suffer any loss due to reliance upon any misrepresentation that I have made on this application, and/or in criminal penalties including, but not limited to, fine or imprisonment or both under the provisions of Title 18, United States Code, Sec. 1001, et seq.; (2) the loan requested pursuant to this application (the "Loan") will be secured by a mortgage or deed of trust on the property described in this application; (3) the property will not be used for any illegal or prohibited purpose or use; (4) all statements made in this application are made for the purpose of obtaining a residential mortgage loan; (5) the property will be occupied as indicated in this application; (6) the Lender, its servicers, successors or assigns may retain the original and/or an electronic record of this application, whether or not the Loan is approved; (7) the Lender and its agents, brokers, insurers, servicers, successors, and assigns may continuously rely on the information contained in the application, and I am obligated to amend and/or supplement the information provided in this application if any of the material facts that I have represented herein should change prior to closing of the Loan; (8) in the event that my payments on the Loan become delinquent, the Lender, its servicers, successors or assigns may, in addition to any other rights and remedies that it may have relating to such delinquency, report my name and account information to one or more consumer reporting agencies; (9) ownership of the Loan and/or administration of the Loan account may be transferred with such notice as may be required by law; (10) neither Lender nor its agents, brokers, insurers, servicers, successors or assigns has made any representation or warranty, express or implied, to me regarding the property or the condition or value of the property; and (11) my transmission of this application as an "electronic record" containing my "electronic signature," as those terms are defined in applicable federal and/or state laws (excluding audio and video recordings), or my facsimile transmission of this application containing a facsimile of my signature, shall be as effective, enforceable and valid as if a paper version of this application were delivered containing my original written signature.

Acknowledgement. Each of the undersigned hereby acknowledges that any owner of the Loan, its servicers, successors and assigns, may verify or reverify any information contained in this application or obtain any information or data relating to the Loan, for any legitimate business purpose through any source, including a source named in this application or a consumer reporting agency.

Borrower's Signature X	Date	Co-Borrower's Signature X	Date

X. INFORMATION FOR GOVERNMENT MONITORING PURPOSES

The following information is requested by the Federal Government for certain types of loans related to a dwelling in order to monitor the lender's compliance with equal credit opportunity, fair housing and home mortgage disclosure laws. You are not required to furnish this information, but are encouraged to do so. The law provides that a lender may not discriminate either on the basis of this information, or on whether you choose to furnish it. If you furnish the information, please provide both ethnicity and race. For race, you may check more than one designation. If you do not furnish ethnicity, race, or sex, under Federal regulations, this lender is required to note the information on the basis of visual observation and surname if you have made this application in person. If you do not wish to furnish the information, please check the box below. (Lender must review the above material to assure that the disclosures satisfy all requirements to which the lender is subject under applicable state law for the particular type of loan applied for.)

BORROWER ☐ I do not wish to furnish this information	**CO-BORROWER** ☐ I do not wish to furnish this information
Ethnicity: ☐ Hispanic or Latino ☐ Not Hispanic or Latino	**Ethnicity:** ☐ Hispanic or Latino ☐ Not Hispanic or Latino
Race: ☐ American Indian or Alaska Native ☐ Asian ☐ Black or African American ☐ Native Hawaiian or Other Pacific Islander ☐ White	**Race:** ☐ American Indian or Alaska Native ☐ Asian ☐ Black or African American ☐ Native Hawaiian or Other Pacific Islander ☐ White
Sex: ☐ Female ☐ Male	**Sex:** ☐ Female ☐ Male

To be Completed by Interviewer This application was taken by: ☐ Face-to-face interview ☐ Mail ☐ Telephone ☐ Internet	Interviewer's Name (print or type)	Name and Address of Interviewer's Employer
	Interviewer's Signature Date	
	Interviewer's Phone Number (incl. area code)	

CONTINUATION SHEET/RESIDENTIAL LOAN APPLICATION			
Use this continuation sheet if you need more space to complete the Residential Loan Application. Mark B f or Borrower or C for Co-Borrower.	Borrower:		Agency Case Number:
	Co-Borrower:		Lender Case Number:

I/We fully understand that it is a Federal crime punishable by fine or imprisonment, or both, to knowingly make any false statements concerning any of the above facts as applicable under the provisions of Title 18, United States Code, Section 1001, et seq.

Borrower's Signature	Date	Co-Borrower's Signature	Date
X		X	

Freddie Mac Form 65   7/05   Page 5 of 5   Fannie Mae Form 1003   7/05

UNIFORM RESIDENTIAL LOAN APPLICATION (1003)

The Lender uses this form to record relevant financial information about an applicant who applies for a one- to a four-family mortgage.

Instructions

The Lender may accept applications taken during a face-to-face interview, over the telephone, through the mail, or via the Internet. The Lender should complete all blanks and attach any separate exhibits, details, or statements relevant to underwriting the mortgage. The Borrower (s) must sign the original application when it is completed. If the application is taken over the telephone or via the Internet, the Borrower (s) must sign the completed application as soon as possible. However, an electronic signature or facsimile of the Borrower's signature is acceptable as indicated in the "Acknowledgment and Agreement" section of the application. The Lender should retain the original application with the supporting information provided by the Borrower (s). Before or at the loan closing, the Borrower (s) must sign the final application that the Lender prepares based on its verification of the information that the Borrower (s) provided in the original application.

The instructions at the top of Form 1003 are consistent with the permissible inquiries that creditors can make under the Equal Credit Opportunity Act (ECOA). Although ECOA permits the Lender in a community property state to obtain information regarding the liabilities of a borrower's spouse even though he or she is not applying for the mortgage and his or her income will not be considered for loan qualification purposes, we do require the Lender to obtain the information.

Statement at the top of the form:

We recognize that the introductory paragraph of Form 1003 differs slightly from the preceding paragraph in the Uniform Residential Loan Application found on Freddie Mac's website, Freddie Mac Form 65. However, because we have determined that these differences are not material, Fannie Mae will deem either version to comply with our requirements for the use of the Uniform Residential Loan Application.

Assets and Liabilities

When the Borrower's and co-borrowers assets and liabilities are not sufficiently joined to make a combined statement meaningful, a separate Statement of Assets and Liabilities (Form 1003A) should be completed for the co-borrower.

Details of Transaction

The purchase price shown on Line "a" under the "Details of Transaction" should not include any discounts or rebates or other allowances paid or allowed to the purchaser. For refinancing, the amount being refinanced should be shown on Line "d" -- Refinance. The figure should include the total amount of all existing liens plus the costs of improvements that have been -- or will be -- made. Lines "a", "b", and "c" should not be used to describe a refinance transaction.

Declarations

Noncitizen Applicants: If an applicant indicates in his response to Question J that he is not a U.S. citizen, and also indicates in his response to Question K that he is not a permanent resident alien, the Lender may wish to ask whether he is a nonpermanent resident alien or otherwise is lawfully present in the United States.

Information for Government Monitoring Purposes

This section is included to aid the federal government in monitoring compliance with equal credit opportunity, fair housing, and home mortgage disclosure laws. Supplying this information is strictly voluntary on the part of the applicant. Still, lenders should ask all applicants to provide it, including those who apply by telephone and through the Internet and should describe the reason for collecting this data. Race and ethnicity are separate categories, and although the Lender should ask applicants to furnish information for both, applicants may provide one but not the other. There is no longer a place for applicants to indicate race as "Other," but applicants may check as many races as they apply.

The Home Mortgage Disclosure Act and its implementation Regulation C require Lenders to collect sex, race, and ethnicity data on all applications.

When an application is taken in person, and an applicant elects not to provide some or all of this information, federal law requires the Lender to note the applicant's sex, ethnicity, and race on the form, based on the Lender's visual observation or the applicant's surname. To aid in identifying applicants who may be of Hispanic ethnicity and who elect not to self-identify, the Lender may wish to consult the list of Spanish surnames developed by the U.S. Bureau of the Census. Furthermore, the Lender may wish to advise the applicant that he may complete or change the information in this section after the application is approved, at any time up until closing.

To Be Completed By Interviewer

The interviewer must complete this portion of the form to indicate the method used to make the application and provide the name and telephone number of the interviewer and their employer's name and address.

To Be Completed By Loan Originator (for PDF dated 06/09 for mortgage loans applications taken on or after January 1, 2010)

The loan originator must complete this portion of the form to indicate the method used to make the application and provide the loan originator's name, ID, telephone number, and employer's name, company ID, and address.

Continuation Sheet/Residential Loan Application

Lenders may amend this section by including space to evidence intent to apply for joint credit. Other approaches, such as including this information on a separate document, are also acceptable to Fannie Mae, provided they meet the requirements of applicable law. Lenders should consult counsel to determine their alternatives.

Special Notice for Balloon Mortgages

For each balloon mortgage, the Lender must insert a special notice regarding the nature of the balloon features on Form 1003 or in a separate attachment to the form.
The Borrower (s) must sign the attachment if an attachment is used. The following language must be inserted, using capital letters:

"THIS LOAN MUST EITHER BE PAID IN FULL AT MATURITY OR REFINANCED TO
A MARKET-LEVEL FIXED-RATE MORTGAGE. YOU MUST REPAY THE ENTIRE
PRINCIPAL BALANCE OF THE LOAN AND UNPAID INTEREST THEN DUE IF YOU
DO NOT QUALIFY FOR THE CONDITIONAL RIGHT TO REFINANCE AS
SPECIFIED IN THE NOTE ADDENDUM AND MORTGAGE RIDER. THE LENDER IS
UNDER NO OBLIGATION TO REFINANCE THE LOAN IF QUALIFICATION CONDITIONS ARE
NOT MET. YOU WILL, THEREFORE, BE REQUIRED TO MAKE
PAYMENT OUT OF OTHER ASSETS THAT YOU MAY OWN, OR YOU WILL HAVE

TO FIND A LENDER, WHICH MAY BE THE LENDER YOU HAVE THIS LOAN WITH, WILLING TO LEND YOU THE MONEY. IF YOU REFINANCE THIS LOAN AT MATURITY, YOU MAY HAVE TO PAY SOME OR ALL OF THE CLOSING COSTS NORMALLY ASSOCIATED WITH A NEW LOAN EVEN IF YOU OBTAIN REFINANCING."

Every Mortgage Company, every bank, and every Lender have guidelines to follow for the government, whether the loan is Federal Housing Administration (FHA), Veterans Administration (VA), Conventional or Rural Development (USDA). The actual institution you are dealing with may have overlays which mean (Their own set of guidelines) also on top of the normal guidelines that we must all follow.

An important fact to always remember is that the person you meet to do your loan application is not the one who approves your loan, they are the fuel that powers the engine by gathering and structuring the file, but they are not the final say. They are simply the beginning of the process. There will be a loan processor who puts all the information together to submit to the underwriting team.

THE UNDERWRITER is the one who approves suspends (meaning something in the file gives them concern, but at that point, they are willing to work and see if they can obtain clarity). They can also delay (reject) the file. This is who must go through the file to make sure everything lines up and all guidelines are met.

I say delay. I don't use the other word (reject) because I genuinely believe that everyone should have a chance at homeownership. Some people just need a little more work than others. Patience and persistence will get you to your goal. (SET YOUR GOALS)

You also must own your own issues and find someone who can help get you through them; the only reason I am good at helping others is that I myself have been there and know how it feels to have the feeling of hopelessness behind what life threw my way.

All the above information is vital to have when you are thinking of calling a Real Estate Agent to begin looking for a home. I said to call a Real Estate Agent because they have the knowledge, experience, and wisdom you need, and let's not forget the access to knowing what properties are available in the real estate market.

THE PROCESS

Different Internet sites are usually not up to date, and the site cannot negotiate a good deal for you. Realtors know what the Seller can pay on your behalf and what you must have to meet those pesky guidelines.

Please take it from someone who has been in this business a mighty long time. It just works better when you work with a realtor, and you do the preparation work.

You must be patient with the process and know that every case is unique. Just because something worked for one person does not mean that it will work for you.

Remember, when you decide to tell people you are purchasing a home, everyone will have all kinds of advice, even if it is not true or accurate. Everyone wants you to think they got a better deal than you are getting, or they simply know everything. But if Real Estate or Mortgages is not what they do for a living, nicely let them know you are working with a team of professionals.

I closed on a loan for 1 month. The Borrower walked in my office, referred to me by a different person. Still, the lady got frustrated through the process because she had some work to do. She began to tell me about a friend who closed on their home for over a month, and she did not go through any of this. So, I informed her that I could not answer that case because I did not do the loan. Her next appointment to bring in conditions her friend came with her, WELL, my client from the previous month. (SMALL WORLD)
She looked as if she had seen a Ghost because none of what she said was true. Her case was worse than the case at hand. So, when she walked in, I said OMG, you are the friend. How is your new home? She went stuttering, and the now Borrower knew something was not right. I never said anything, and you know she called and asked me, but my answer was, let's just focus on you and your dealer. 2 weeks later, she closed her deal.

MAKE YOUR LIST OF WHO NOT TO LISTEN TO DURING THIS PROCESS!!!
THE BEST POLICY IS TO MOVE IN SILENCE

ANALYZE YOUR THOUGHTS

Before making an appointment with someone, ask yourself a few questions you may even want to ask the Mortgage expert you chose to work with some of the following questions also. This will allow you to make an informative decision.

1. Do you want to be a homeowner with all the responsibilities of homeownership? (Repairs, grass & Insurance)
2. What is the advantage of being a homeowner versus being a renter? (Tax write off, a sense of accomplishment)
3. What would be the disadvantage of becoming a homeowner?
4. Can I afford to purchase a home? (How much can I afford)
5. Is my income stable and steady enough? (Will I continue to increase my revenue)
6. Take time to analyze your current expenses. (Bills, credit cards, car notes, ETC)
7. Will my credit be a problem? (If so what can I do to increase it)
8. Do I have any judgments or tax liens or Bankruptcies?
9. Can I afford the down payment?
10. Can I withdraw out of my 401k plan?
11. What is my buying power? How much can I buy?
12. Where do I want to live?
13. What is included in my monthly note?

Stay focused and write things down to understand what is going on. I suggest getting a notebook when you start the process and every time you speak with someone, write it down, (meaning) write what they said, who you spoke to their names.

If you think of any questions and you can speak to anyone at the time, write them down so you can ask, remember you are making one of the most significant investments of your life. You must have a clear understanding of what you are doing so obtain as much wisdom about the process as possible.

Important Note:
The market and the guidelines and programs change all the time, rates change daily and sometimes 2 & 3 times a day.

** REMEMBER guidelines are the same in the mortgage Industry, everywhere you go. Some lenders have more overlays than others, meaning stricter restrictions imposed by their institution (Meaning the level of risk they are willing to take).

MAKING THE CALL

When you make the call, the first thing they will want to do is **RUN YOUR CREDIT REPORT** to see what your history looks like and the credit score from all 3 major credit banks, Equifax, Transunion, and Experian.

In the mortgage industry, we use **FICO scores which range from 300 to 850. There is what they call Vantage Score: and this is the one that people such as the online credit people use, but it is not the system for purchasing homes or cars. The scores differ drastically most times.**

A FICO score is a three-digit number based on the information in your credit reports. It helps lenders determine how likely you are to repay a loan. This, in turn, affects how much you can borrow, how many months you have to repay, and how much it will cost (the interest rate.) Only FICO scores are created by Fiat Isaac Corporation and are used by over 90% of the top lenders when making lending decisions.

Why? Because FICO Scores are the industry standard for making accurate and fair decisions about creditworthiness. They help millions of people get the credit they need for a home loan, a new car, and special purchases.

This component says whether you can proceed or you have some work to do first. The Lender you are working with will be looking for several things during the initial process; they will analyze your credit report from top to bottom.

Looking at your credit scores, you have 3 different scoring banks, Transunion, Equifax, Experian. The middle score determines how much you can borrow against your ratios. The higher the score, the more leanness they will have. Instead of being stuck to 43% on FHA, you may go as high as 57% on the back end (Debt to income). Some lenders will allow you to be approved with scores as low as 585; however, the rates are higher than if you work and achieve a 620 or better. Please keep in mind this is strictly on the owner-occupied property; investment purchasing, your score must be at least a 660 or higher.

Your credit score is a statistical way to predict the likelihood of repaying and managing your credit obligation. We all know things happen in life; you will need good explanations and documentation if possible.

Your score is based on the information that is reported in the credit agencies Equifax, Transunion, and Experian. They are calculated based on:

Previous credit history
Current credit history / If you pay on time
Amount of time credit has been in established
Inquiries in the last 12 months
You currently have the type of credit cards, bank loans, auto loans, etc.
Balances compared to the credit limit that was granted on the account.
Your scores determine how much you can purchase. The scores keep your qualifying debt to income ratios in line.

So yes, scores matter.
FHA ratios are 31/41 however, Lenders do stretch w/ scores over 620
USDA ratios are 29/41 with no stretch
VA ratios are 41% with stretches with scores over 620 + residual income.
Conventional, which is also known as conforming, is 43 Little stretch
Everything has exceptions w/ compensating factors.
You can increase your buying power by doing a few things:
Reduce your monthly debt, bring your available credit down below 30% on credit card accounts, and wait until your income increases. Get someone to cosign for you.

The mortgage professional you choose should be able to help you in making an informed decision.

They will also be aware of any mortgage products or special programs offered in your city, which will help you purchase your home.

Special programs are not always available, and it depends on what city or state you live in and who has to grant money at the time.

YOUR IDENTITY

They must make sure your name is spelled right and ask questions such as are you married, single, divorced. Be honest because when the Title Company runs your name, your status will come up throughout the process.

This is very important because if you live in a community property state, the Lender is required to run the spouse's credit report. Also, FHA requires you to qualify with all debt even though any unmanageable debt they may have will not stop your process. It will make your qualification different.

There is a document called and interventions that can be signed to make the property your sole property and not hold the unmanageable debt against you. If you are a male and a Junior or Senior, you must disclose this fact as it is essential because a father or a son could have debt that appears on your credit history and will need to be removed. Remember, your credit is put into a system by people, and sometimes some mistakes occur.

Next, does the name and social security number match? Believe it or not, this is a mistake that happens more often than we realize:

(IE) My Mom's credit had been infiltrated because she had the same exact name, first and last as an individual who lives in a totally different city, their social security numbers were off by 1 digit, birth dates were different; however, my Mom had about 6 accounts reporting on her report that were not hers. We had to write to each creditor and all 3 credit banks and copy her Social Security number to get the items removed. It took about 3 months to have this done, but I was persistent. The follow-up is very important. Nothing will happen if you do not follow up because it is not important to the creditor; it must be **important** to you.

The Lender must check all documents that have your identity on it: Driver's license, social security card, tax documents, check stubs if anything appears different, you must give a written explanation and, in some cases, provide documentation.

Following items to be reviewed:

THE PROCESS

Your address for the last 2 years is what they verify. If any addresses appear on the credit report that you did not disclose to us or do not show up on any of your documentation, you will have to write a letter of explanation.

They check your address against your credit, identification card, check stubs, bank statements, and tax returns. The title company will also review these facts.

ACCOUNTS

Current open accounts that you are paying every month. They are looking at your balance compared to what you can Borrower; this significantly impacts your credit scores. (ie) your credit line is $5,000, and you owe $5,000. This will lower your score.

The rule of thumb is you should never owe more than 30% of what they have approved you to Borrower. Remember late is anything over 30days; you MUST pay within the 30-day limit if the bill is due on the 15th of the month; make sure it is paid on or before the 14th of the next month. Underwriters do NOT like to see 30-day overdue payments on any tradeline. If you have one, you must document and explain why it was late. Sometimes it could be an error, but you must produce documentation to be removed from your history. They are also looking at the length of time you have had the account. This will affect the score also.

Looking at student loans and their statutes at the time of loan application, each program has different guidelines to follow FHA. If you do not have a fixed payment, they will count 1% of the loan amount against you. In most cases, this will lower your qualifying amount, or possibly you can be denied, but had you taken the time to make a call, the outcome could be different.

Please pick up the phone and make the call, find out how to obtain the Standardized fixed payment on the loan or loans, and obtain it in writing to make your loan work.

They will offer you several other programs, but if it is not a FIXED payment, the underwriter will not use it. They will go back to the .5% rule.

Conventional loans use whatever the payment is that appears on the credit report; they only allow this practice today. If the credit report states zero payment, that's what they will use.

This is all part of the process of being approved for your Real Estate purchase. Still looking at your credit, they then move to any collection account that appears on the report; when analyzing the collection accounts, we must look at the length and the balance that is in collections; some will have to be paid off or settled in full, others may not be required.

Charge Off account and now very rarely get touched by underwriters but remember it is within their discussion if you must pay the debt.

THE PROCESS

ALL judgment, tax liens MUST be paid no exceptions because if they allow you to close the judgment or lien will prime the mortgage and take first place, let's face it no one loaning you money wants to take a 2nd lien unless that is their purpose when originating the loan in the beginning. Once the judgment or lien is paid in full, we need the release from the courts to get the credit agencies to update your credit file.

Please note there is a lot to this qualifying process. It is not just throwing the loan up against the wall and hoping it sticks; we must paint the picture and make it clean.
When you have a bankruptcy in your history, you need to have a full copy of the bankruptcy papers and the discharge.

Chapter 7 full bankruptcy / Chapter 13 reorganizing
- There will be stipulations if you fall under bankruptcy.
- 2-year period with no late payments from your discharge
- Chapter 13, you must be paid halfway through.
- Please obtain permission from the trustee to enter into a purchase, a letter from them stating where you began, the balance, and the monthly payment.

Inquiries within the last 12 months must be explained, and, in the letter, it must state if you have obtained any new credit that may not appear on the credit report.

INCOME VERIFICATION

Gross Monthly Income: If the net cash flow for an investment property is a positive number, it should be listed as "net rental income." If it is a negative number, it must be included in the applicant's monthly obligations. Suppose the property is a two- to the four-unit property for which the applicant occupies one of the units as a principal residence. In that case, the monthly rental income should be listed as "net rental income."

Combined Monthly Housing Expense: The present monthly housing expenses for the Borrower and the co-borrower should be listed on a combined basis. The proposed monthly housing expense for a two- to four-unit property where the applicant will occupy a unit as a principal residence should reflect the monthly payment (PITIA) for the subject property. The present monthly housing expense should reflect the applicant's principal residence for all one- to four-unit investment properties.

Employed borrowers need to bring in the last 2 check stubs on the check stubs will be looking at several things:

1. If you are hourly or salary
2. If you do overtime, bonuses, commission, or stipends, and are consistent, have you received it for the last 2 years (a very important fact) in the qualifying process.
3. Look at your deductions to ensure you do not have extra bills that may not be reported to the credit agencies.

Doing this, it gives us an idea of your monthly income.

TAX RETURNS

Tax returns for the past 2 years are vital because if you are employed and receive check stubs and w'2 forms 9 times out of 10, you have NO legit tax deductions; if you take deductions, it will hinder you from purchasing or making any Real Estate transactions. The processor will take the deduction from your income and average what you filed over the last 2 years to give you an income. IE, you make $40,000 per year, which will give us $3333.33 per month but suppose you wrote your income down to 18,500 after deductions. You now have 1541.66 per month in income. Getting a refund at the end of the year can hurt you when trying to make moves in your life.

Self-Employed Borrower, you need your tax returns from the last 2 years and a current profit and loss statement. It is so essential how you file and what write-offs you take. This practice may help you not have to pay the IRS, but I can promise you it will hinder you from purchasing a home because every write-off is a deduction from your income.

Once you have evaluated all the information above, answered all the questions, and had your consultation with a mortgage professional, you are now ready and equipped with what you need to move forward in purchasing your new home.

This means you now have considered and know where your money will come from to help with the down payment and closing cost to purchase. Keep in mind the Seller can help with closing costs. There is no guarantee that they will pay the price, but it is negotiable in every contract.

FHA sellers can pay up to 6% of the borrower's closing cost; your down payment is 3.5% which must be your funds, by way of bank accounts, retirement funds, gifts, grants.

A seller can pay up to 4% of the Borrower's closing cost; no down payment is required. Conventional sellers can pay up to 3% of the borrower's closing cost; your down payment is at least 5% down of your funds. It could be as much as 20% down.

USDA sellers can pay up to 6% of the borrower's closing cost; your down payment is zero.

You have turned in all information, and the Lender you have chosen has prequalified you and is ready to issue a pre-approval letter to the agent; this lets them know they have a ready borrower. Most Agents will not show you property unless you can get them the letter. This is because most Listing agents and sellers want to see the letter immediately and will not accept a contract if one is not provided.

Now you are ready to begin shopping for a home; my advice to everyone taking this journey is to get with a real estate agent; do not try and accomplish this on your own. The Realtor has been trained to help you with your journey. They are professionals who have the resources and tools to find all homes on the market. Remember they work with you and for you at NO cost to you; the Seller pays agents once the loan is closed.

The agent will have questions for you also; think about the following so you will be prepared, and they can help you better:

1. Where would you like to live? LOCATION
2. What is important to you about your neighborhood?
3. What type of property do you want?
4. Do you want a new construction one ready to move in or a rehabilitation home?
5. What size home are you looking for?

All the above questions will help them to find you the home of your dreams. Now the search begins.

NEGOTIATING THE PURCHASE CONTRACT IS THE NEXT STEP IN YOUR PROCESS

Your Realtor we pull comps in the area to determine what you should offer on the property; certain things are a factor when making your offer:

1. Sales price compared to what you want to offer someone for their home. The listing agent has often done their homework and has the property listed correctly but do your research.
2. Do you want the Seller to pay any of your closing costs, this needs to be stated in the initial offer?
3. How long before you can close, you should check with the Lender who is going to obtain the mortgage for you. This is very important because if the date is not met, the contract is now open and needs an addendum to extend the closing date, or either party can back out of the transaction.
4. Are there any points associated with the loan or just the origination fee?
5. Are there any repairs that will need to be done to the property you ask the Seller to do before closing on the home?
6. The type of financing needs to be stipulated in the purchase agreement; this gives everybody some idea of what will be going on during the process.
7. If anything is being left in the property, that should be on an addendum to the purchase contract.
8. Remember, a deposit is required to hold the property off the market.
9. Everyone must agree and sign the contract to make it valid and binding.

The next step you are now turned back over to the Mortgage Company to begin the process of disclosing to you all the particulars of the deal. Such as how much you will need to close they cannot give you the figures till the contract is accepted. Once you sign all disclosures, the file is processed; you then will sign your initial disclosures within 72 hours from the mortgage company receiving the signed contract and all addendums to the agreement. They will place the file into an investor's system and submit it to the setup team so that the file can be put into the underwriter for approval.

The setup team will go through the file to see if the processor has missed anything they can catch before placing the file in line for Underwriting. Underwriting can take anywhere from 24 hours to 1 week, depending on how backed up they are in Underwriting and what time of year it is. Certain times of the year are busier than others, and other times of the year are vacation and holiday time. Patience is required when going through this process.

The purpose of this summary appraisal report is to provide the lender/client with an accurate, and adequately supported. opinion of the market value of the subject property.

S U B J E C T	Property Address	City	State	Zip Code
	Borrower	Owner of Public Record	County	
	Legal Description			
	Assessor's Parcel #	Tax Year	R.E. Taxes $	
	Neighborhood Name	Map Reference	Census Tract	
	Occupant ☐ Owner ☐ Tenant ☐ Vacant	Special Assessments $	☐ PUD HOA $	☐ per year ☐ per month
	Property Rights Appraised ☐ Fee Simple ☐ Leasehold ☐ Other (describe)			
	Assignment Type ☐ Purchase Transaction ☐ Refinance Transaction ☐ Other (describe)			
	Lender/Client	Address		
	Is the subject property currently offered for sale or has it been offered for sale in the twelve months prior to the effective date of this appraisal? ☐ Yes ☐ No			
	Report data source(s) used, offering price(s), and date(s).			

C O N T R A C T	I ☐ did ☐ did not analyze the contract for sale for the subject purchase transaction. Explain the results of the analysis of the contract for sale or why the analysis was not performed.
	Contract Price $ Date of Contract Is the property seller the owner of public record? ☐ Yes ☐ No Data Source(s)
	Is there any financial assistance (loan charges, sale concessions, gift or downpayment assistance, etc.) to be paid by any party on behalf of the borrower? ☐ Yes ☐ No
	If Yes, report the total dollar amount and describe the items to be paid.

Note: Race and the racial composition of the neighborhood are not appraisal factors.

Neighborhood Characteristics			One-Unit Housing Trends			One-Unit Housing		Present Land Use %	
Location ☐ Urban ☐ Suburban ☐ Rural			Property Values ☐ Increasing ☐ Stable ☐ Declining			PRICE	AGE	One-Unit	%
Built-Up ☐ Over 75% ☐ 25-75% ☐ Under 25%			Demand/Supply ☐ Shortage ☐ In Balance ☐ Over Supply			$ (000)	(yrs)	2-4 Unit	%
Growth ☐ Rapid ☐ Stable ☐ Slow			Marketing Time ☐ Under 3 mths ☐ 3-6 mths ☐ Over 6 mths			Low		Multi-Family	%
Neighborhood Boundaries						High		Commercial	%
						Pred.		Other	%

N E I G H B O R H O O D

Neighborhood Description

Market Conditions (including support for the above conclusions)

Dimensions	Area	Shape	View
Specific Zoning Classification	Zoning Description		

Zoning Compliance ☐ Legal ☐ Legal Nonconforming (Grandfathered Use) ☐ No Zoning ☐ Illegal (describe)

Is the highest and best use of the subject property as improved (or as proposed per plans and specifications) the present use? ☐ Yes ☐ No If No, describe

Utilities	Public	Other (describe)		Public	Other (describe)	Off-site Improvements—Type	Public	Private
Electricity	☐	☐	Water	☐	☐	Street	☐	☐
Gas	☐	☐	Sanitary Sewer	☐	☐	Alley	☐	☐

S I T E

FEMA Special Flood Hazard Area ☐ Yes ☐ No FEMA Flood Zone   FEMA Map #   FEMA Map Date

Are the utilities and off-site improvements typical for the market area? ☐ Yes ☐ No If No, describe

Are there any adverse site conditions or external factors (easements, encroachments, environmental conditions, land uses, etc.)? ☐ Yes ☐ No If Yes, describe

General Description	Foundation	Exterior Description materials/condition	Interior materials/condition
Units ☐ One ☐ One with Accessory Unit	☐ Concrete Slab ☐ Crawl Space	Foundation Walls	Floors
# of Stories	☐ Full Basement ☐ Partial Basement	Exterior Walls	Walls
Type ☐ Det. ☐ Att. ☐ S-Det./End Unit	Basement Area sq. ft.	Roof Surface	Trim/Finish
☐ Existing ☐ Proposed ☐ Under Const.	Basement Finish %	Gutters & Downspouts	Bath Floor
Design (Style)	☐ Outside Entry/Exit ☐ Sump Pump	Window Type	Bath Wainscot
Year Built	Evidence of ☐ Infestation	Storm Sash/Insulated	Car Storage ☐ None
Effective Age (Yrs)	☐ Dampness ☐ Settlement	Screens	☐ Driveway # of Cars
Attic ☐ None	Heating ☐ FWA ☐ HWBB ☐ Radiant	Amenities ☐ Woodstove(s) #	Driveway Surface
☐ Drop Stair ☐ Stairs	☐ Other Fuel	☐ Fireplace(s) # ☐ Fence	☐ Garage # of Cars
☐ Floor ☐ Scuttle	Cooling ☐ Central Air Conditioning	☐ Patio/Deck ☐ Porch	☐ Carport # of Cars
☐ Finished ☐ Heated	☐ Individual ☐ Other	☐ Pool ☐ Other	☐ Att. ☐ Det. ☐ Built-in

I M P R O V E M E N T S

Appliances ☐ Refrigerator ☐ Range/Oven ☐ Dishwasher ☐ Disposal ☐ Microwave ☐ Washer/Dryer ☐ Other (describe)

Finished area **above grade** contains: Rooms   Bedrooms   Bath(s)   Square Feet of Gross Living Area Above Grade

Additional features (special energy efficient items, etc.)

Describe the condition of the property (including needed repairs, deterioration. renovations, remodeling, etc.).

Are there any physical deficiencies or adverse conditions that affect the livability, soundness, or structural integrity of the property? ☐ Yes ☐ No If Yes, describe

Does the property generally conform to the neighborhood (functional utility, style, condition, use, construction, etc.)? ☐ Yes ☐ No If No, describe

THE PROCESS

| There are | comparable properties currently offered for sale in the subject neighborhood ranging in price from $ | | to $ | . |
| There are | comparable sales in the subject neighborhood within the past twelve months ranging in sale price from $ | | to $ | . |

FEATURE	SUBJECT	COMPARABLE SALE # 1		COMPARABLE SALE # 2		COMPARABLE SALE # 3	
Address							
Proximity to Subject							
Sale Price	$		$		$		$
Sale Price/Gross Liv. Area	$ sq. ft.	$ sq. ft.		$ sq. ft.		$ sq. ft.	
Data Source(s)							
Verification Source(s)							
VALUE ADJUSTMENTS	DESCRIPTION	DESCRIPTION	+(-) $ Adjustment	DESCRIPTION	+(-) $ Adjustment	DESCRIPTION	+(-) $ Adjustment
Sale or Financing Concessions							
Date of Sale/Time							
Location							
Leasehold/Fee Simple							
Site							
View							
Design (Style)							
Quality of Construction							
Actual Age							
Condition							
Above Grade	Total Bdrms. Baths	Total Bdrms. Baths		Total Bdrms. Baths		Total Bdrms. Baths	
Room Count							
Gross Living Area	sq. ft.	sq. ft.		sq. ft.		sq. ft.	
Basement & Finished Rooms Below Grade							
Functional Utility							
Heating/Cooling							
Energy Efficient Items							
Garage/Carport							
Porch/Patio/Deck							
Net Adjustment (Total)		☐ + ☐ -	$	☐ + ☐ -	$	☐ + ☐ -	$
Adjusted Sale Price of Comparables		Net Adj. % Gross Adj. %	$	Net Adj. % Gross Adj. %	$	Net Adj. % Gross Adj. %	$

I ☐ did ☐ did not research the sale or transfer history of the subject property and comparable sales. If not, explain

My research ☐ did ☐ did not reveal any prior sales or transfers of the subject property for the three years prior to the effective date of this appraisal.
Data source(s)

My research ☐ did ☐ did not reveal any prior sales or transfers of the comparable sales for the year prior to the date of sale of the comparable sale.
Data source(s)

Report the results of the research and analysis of the prior sale or transfer history of the subject property and comparable sales (report additional prior sales on page 3).

ITEM	SUBJECT	COMPARABLE SALE # 1	COMPARABLE SALE # 2	COMPARABLE SALE # 3
Date of Prior Sale/Transfer				
Price of Prior Sale/Transfer				
Data Source(s)				
Effective Date of Data Source(s)				

Analysis of prior sale or transfer history of the subject property and comparable sales

Summary of Sales Comparison Approach

Indicated Value by Sales Comparison Approach $

Indicated Value by: Sales Comparison Approach $ Cost Approach (if developed) $ Income Approach (if developed) $

This appraisal is made ☐ "as is", ☐ subject to completion per plans and specifications on the basis of a hypothetical condition that the improvements have been completed, ☐ subject to the following repairs or alterations on the basis of a hypothetical condition that the repairs or alterations have been completed, or ☐ subject to the following required inspection based on the extraordinary assumption that the condition or deficiency does not require alteration or repair:

Based on a complete visual inspection of the interior and exterior areas of the subject property, defined scope of work, statement of assumptions and limiting conditions, and appraiser's certification, my (our) opinion of the market value, as defined, of the real property that is the subject of this report is
$, as of   , which is the date of inspection and the effective date of this appraisal.

Fannie Mae Form 1004   March 2005

ANNA MARIE WILSON

There are	comparable properties currently offered for sale in the subject neighborhood ranging in price from $				to $		
There are	comparable sales in the subject neighborhood within the past twelve months ranging in sale price from $				to $		

FEATURE	SUBJECT	COMPARABLE SALE # 1		COMPARABLE SALE # 2		COMPARABLE SALE # 3	
Address							
Proximity to Subject							
Sale Price	$		$		$		$
Sale Price/Gross Liv. Area	$ sq. ft.	$ sq. ft.		$ sq. ft.		$ sq. ft.	
Data Source(s)							
Verification Source(s)							
VALUE ADJUSTMENTS	DESCRIPTION	DESCRIPTION	+(-) $ Adjustment	DESCRIPTION	+(-) $ Adjustment	DESCRIPTION	+(-) $ Adjustment
Sale or Financing Concessions							
Date of Sale/Time							
Location							
Leasehold/Fee Simple							
Site							
View							
Design (Style)							
Quality of Construction							
Actual Age							
Condition							
Above Grade	Total Bdrms. Baths	Total Bdrms. Baths		Total Bdrms. Baths		Total Bdrms. Baths	
Room Count							
Gross Living Area	sq. ft.	sq. ft.		sq. ft.		sq. ft.	
Basement & Finished Rooms Below Grade							
Functional Utility							
Heating/Cooling							
Energy Efficient Items							
Garage/Carport							
Porch/Patio/Deck							
Net Adjustment (Total)		☐ + ☐ -	$	☐ + ☐ -	$	☐ + ☐ -	$
Adjusted Sale Price of Comparables		Net Adj. % Gross Adj. %	$	Net Adj. % Gross Adj. %	$	Net Adj. % Gross Adj. %	$

I ☐ did ☐ did not research the sale or transfer history of the subject property and comparable sales. If not, explain

My research ☐ did ☐ did not reveal any prior sales or transfers of the subject property for the three years prior to the effective date of this appraisal.
Data source(s)
My research ☐ did ☐ did not reveal any prior sales or transfers of the comparable sales for the year prior to the date of sale of the comparable sale.
Data source(s)
Report the results of the research and analysis of the prior sale or transfer history of the subject property and comparable sales (report additional prior sales on page 3).

ITEM	SUBJECT	COMPARABLE SALE # 1	COMPARABLE SALE # 2	COMPARABLE SALE # 3
Date of Prior Sale/Transfer				
Price of Prior Sale/Transfer				
Data Source(s)				
Effective Date of Data Source(s)				

Analysis of prior sale or transfer history of the subject property and comparable sales

Summary of Sales Comparison Approach

Indicated Value by Sales Comparison Approach $

Indicated Value by: Sales Comparison Approach $ Cost Approach (if developed) $ Income Approach (if developed) $

This appraisal is made ☐ "as is", ☐ subject to completion per plans and specifications on the basis of a hypothetical condition that the improvements have been completed, ☐ subject to the following repairs or alterations on the basis of a hypothetical condition that the repairs or alterations have been completed, or ☐ subject to the following required inspection based on the extraordinary assumption that the condition or deficiency does not require alteration or repair:

Based on a complete visual inspection of the interior and exterior areas of the subject property, defined scope of work, statement of assumptions and limiting conditions, and appraiser's certification, my (our) opinion of the market value, as defined, of the real property that is the subject of this report is $, as of   , which is the date of inspection and the effective date of this appraisal.

35

Fannie Mae Form 1004 March 2005

ABOUT THE AUTHOR

Lincoln Property – 1985 I began working for a property management company. Managing over 200 rental properties throughout New Orleans and the surrounding areas.

In 1990 while still there, I obtained my Real Estate License and then began selling off their homes. I moved over to Prudential Real Estate Co. and began selling houses for several years. A realtor in the office thought I would be good at doing the mortgage end of Real Estate and Referred me to a company where the owner began to teach me the ropes.

Little did I know it would become a passion for helping people with their dreams and vision of homeownership. 1992 I moved to Fleet Mortgage, where I met Carol Johnson, who taught me how to operate in the mortgage industry. Mrs. Johnson stayed with me. She was persistent and determined that I would be one of the best in the business, and I was to understand what you were talking about. She would always say, you will NOT be on the street and not know what you are doing.

Everyone needs a mentor or someone to push them to get it right. I thank God for her, and still today, she is my go-to person when I don't understand something or need to check myself.
I then went to work for City Wide Mortgage Company, wherein in 1998, I was given the honor of being written up in the Essence Magazine for the work I was doing with people who others would reject and turn their back on. I love what I do. It is very fulfilling helping people turn a NO into a YES.

I listen to the new Borrower sitting before me and pay attention no matter how much they want to talk, and whatever they want to talk about, sometimes we must remember it is not about us. When helping others, you must have an ear to listen and slow to speak, be transparent during the initial interview, for they have to have a level of trust that you are the one that will help them and not just throw them to the side.

CPSIA information can be obtained
at www.ICGtesting.com
Printed in the USA
LVHW061200030522
717733LV00013B/460